The thematic elements for making delicious cookies are:

Butter: Butter is the soul of the cookie because butter creates a spongy, melt-in-your-mouth, and seductive aroma. If you use bad butter, your cake will have a fatty aroma, which is very unpleasant.

Review: Since cookies use a lot of flour, it acts as a thickener, making the buttering work easier, more incorporated. In addition, the role of egg white cannot be denied, making the cake more spongy (making air bubbles) and the yolk making the cake more yellow and fragrant with egg aroma. There are also cookies that use only the yolk.

Sweetener quality: Sugar, honey, syrup.. Here we mean the main sweeteners for a single cookie, but of course many other ingredients that make the cake sweeter. Even the powder is involved in its metal, and then there are additional flavor-enhancing ingredients such as jam, dried nuts.

Yellow and white sugar will determine the cake's color, firmness/softness, sweetness and different positions. Basically:

Yellow sugar: makes the cake more yellow, sweeter and has a sour aftertaste at the end of the cake, which has more nostalgia when used. And won't get as hard as white sugar because yellow sugar attracts smaller.

White sugar: whiter cakes, monochromatic cakes and help cakes firmer and drier.

Granulated sugar makes the cake more crispy, granulated sugar makes the cake more crispy.

For soft, spongy, moist cakes, use syrup or honey.

Cakes using 2 sweeteners usually don't last long because the cake is absorbed quickly, so the taste will be distorted quickly. But when you enjoy it, it's really pleasant.

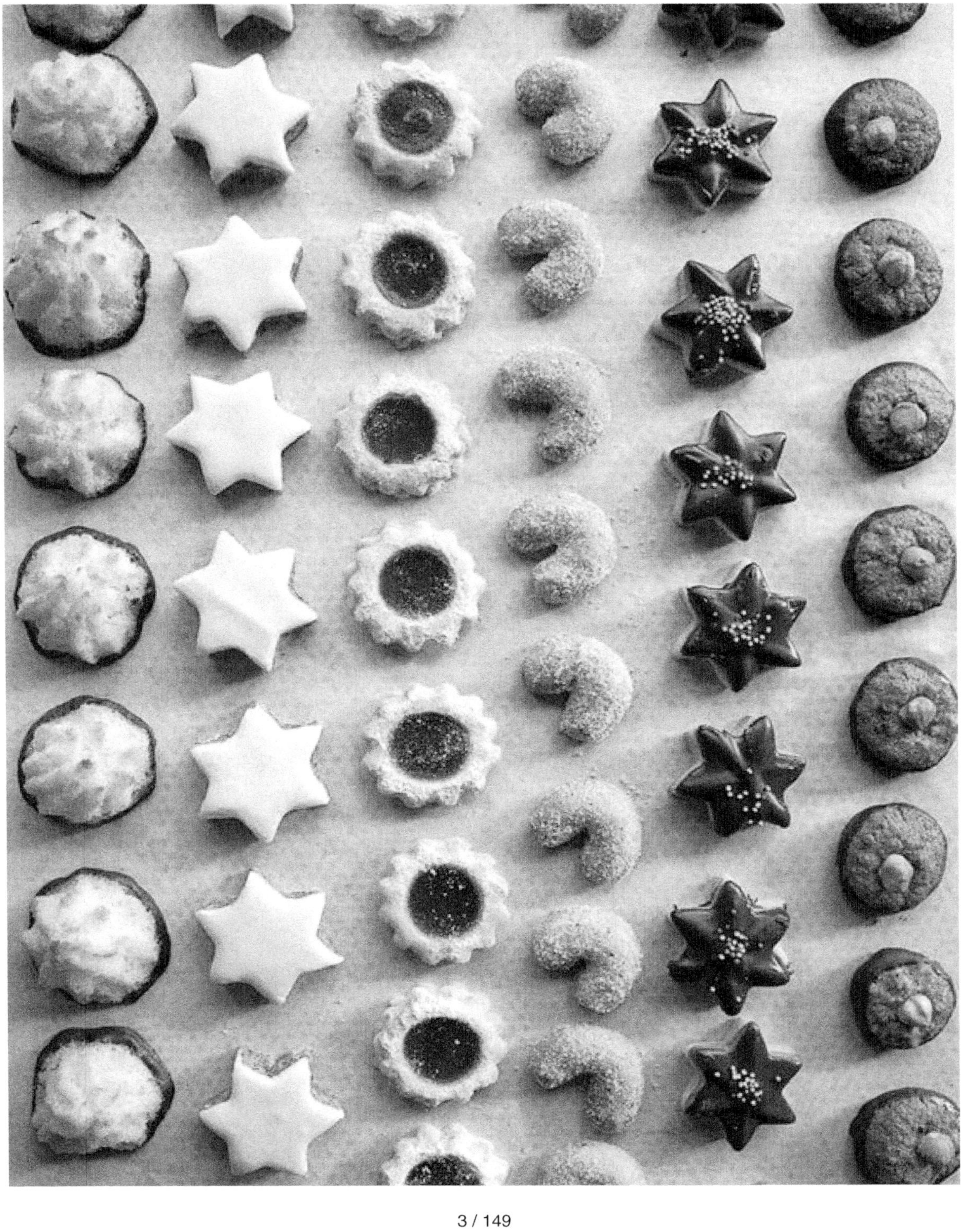

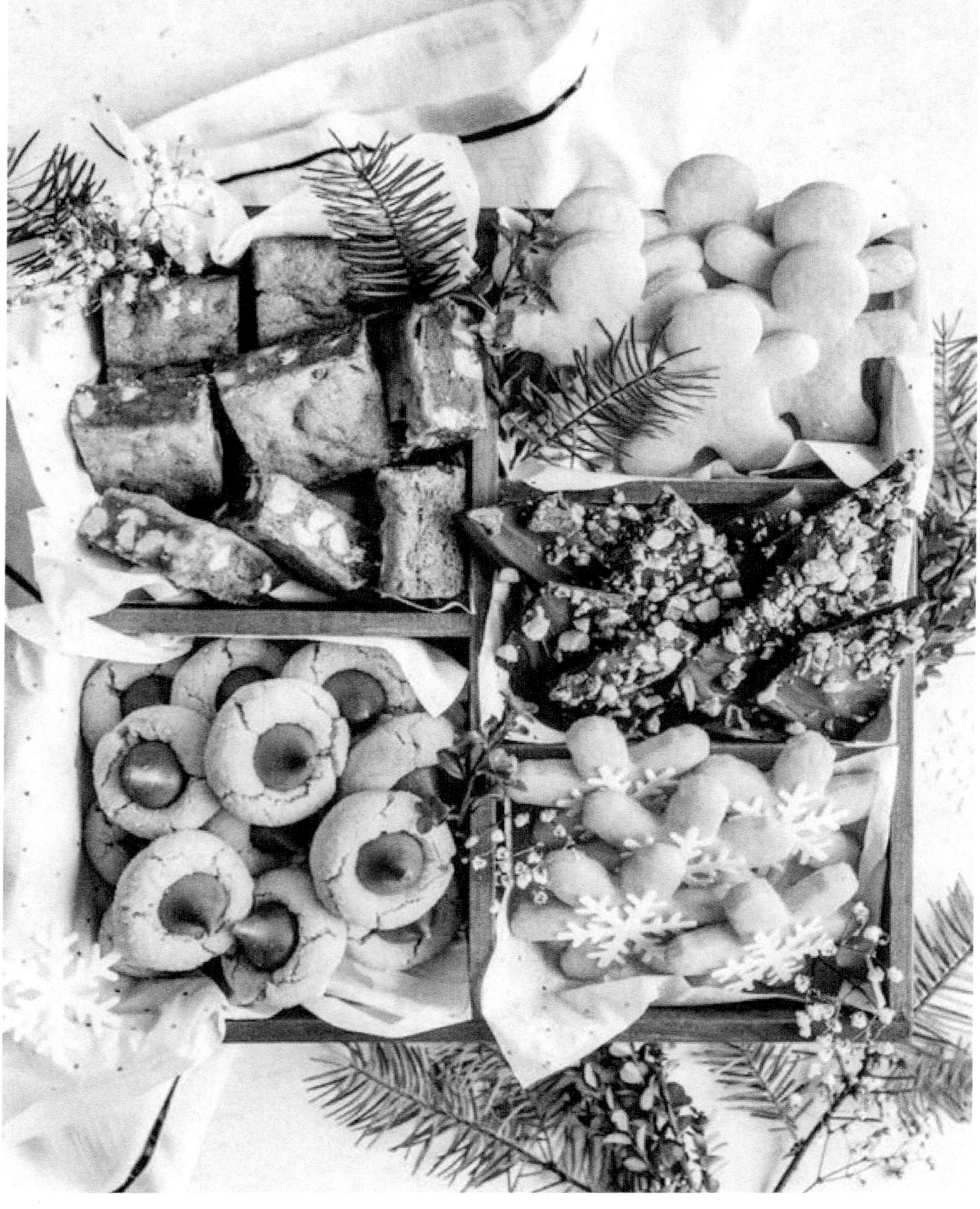

Peanut Butter Cookies

Ingredients for Peanut Butter Cookies

- Butter 225 g
- Peanut butter 300 g
- Shortening 150 g
- White sugar 250 g
- Brown white sugar 250 g
- 3 eggs
- Salt 7 g
- Vanilla extract 10 g
- Baking soda 6 g
- (Salt baking)
- All-purpose flour 500 g
- (Wheat flour number 11)
- Tools: Beater or dough mixer, oven,...

How to make Peanut Butter Cookies

1. Beat the peanut butter mixture
You put 225g butter, 150g shortening, 300g peanut butter, 250g white sugar and 250g brown sugar into the flour mixer. Then mix this powder well.

2. Mix butter with eggs
Then you add 3 berries in turn and beat until the mixture is smooth.

The mixture has been beaten until it is smooth and even, then take it out and knead the dough by hand, then cover and place in the refrigerator for about 30 minutes.

4.Shaping the cake
After 30 minutes of incubating the cake in the refrigerator, take it out and divide the dough into small portions, each about 1 to 1.5 tablespoons of dough, and then roll those dough pieces.

Then use a fork to dip in the flour first to make the non-stick layer, then press the dough ball to flatten it.

5.Baking cake
After shaping the cake, you just need to bring the cake into the oven to bake for 160 degrees for 10 minutes.

After that 10 minutes, take out the cake tray, reverse the cake tray and bake for another 160 degrees for 5 minutes.

6.Finished product
So the peanut cookie is done, when you eat it, you will find the sweetness and fat of peanut butter very attractive, you can use the cake to snack, sip with a cup of tea while bored. Or just chat with friends.

Brownie Cookies Cream

Ingredients for making Brownie Cookies with Cream

- Couverture dark chocolate 115 gr
- Baking powder 50 gr

- Chicken eggs 60 gr
- Brown sugar 65 gr
- Unsalted Butter 55 gr
- Cocoa powder 12 gr
- Starch syrup 55 gr
- Sugar 75 gr
- Baking powder 1 gr
- Baking soda 1 gr
- Gelatin 5 gr
- Vanilla essence 1 gr
- Water 30 gr

Implementation tools
Oven, whisk, mixer

How to make Brownie Cookies with soft cream

1. Melt the chocolate mixture
Put in a bowl 115g couverture dark chocolate, 55g unsalted butter, then heat on a water bath until the mixture melts.

2. Whip the egg mixture
Put in a new bowl 60g eggs, 65g brown sugar, then beat the mixture with an electric mixer until it turns ivory white, lift the whisk to flow like a ribbon (Ribbon Stage State) is done.

Outward remittance:

To scramble eggs faster, you can put the bowl of eggs in a pot of warm water until the eggs reach a temperature of 40 degrees Celsius. Then, remove the bowl from the pot and perform the whisking process.

However, you should only warm the eggs to about 40 - 50 degrees Celsius, otherwise the eggs will be overcooked and less fluffy.

3.Mix the chocolate mixture

Add the beaten eggs to the chocolate mixture, then use a spatula to gently mix the mixture from bottom to top.

Bring the spatula to the bottom of the bowl, lift the heavy ingredients, and fold aside. Continue until the mixture is combined.

4.Mix cake dough

Sift 50g baking powder, 10g cocoa powder, 1g baking powder, 1g baking soda into the chocolate mixture.

Use a spatula to stir in one direction until the mixture is smooth.

Then, put the mixture in the refrigerator until it reaches 24 degrees Celsius.

5.Pour the mold and bake the cake

Preheat oven to 180 degrees Celsius for 15 minutes.

Line the baking sheet with parchment paper and place the dough in the mold, then bake at 180 degrees Celsius for 15 minutes.

6.Cooking sugar syrup
Put the pot on the stove, then add 75 grams of sugar, 55 grams of starch syrup, 30 grams of water, and cook over medium heat until the mixture boils about 114 - 118 degrees Celsius.

Note: Do not stir the mixture during the cooking process.
7.Make chocolate sugar ice cream
In a bowl, add sugar syrup, 1g vanilla essence, 5g leaf gelatin and beat with a whisk until the mixture turns white.

Then, add 2g cocoa powder and continue to beat until the mixture is smooth.

8.Pumping cake filling
Pump the sugar cream filling into the inside of the cake and you're done.

9.Finished product
Brownie cookies have a soft, spongy crust, soft marshmallows inside, extremely fun to chew and extremely delicious.

Brownie Cookie Matcha

Ingredients for Brownie Cookie Matcha

- Chocolate 80 gr
- Unsalted butter 30 gr
- 1 egg

- Vanilla essence 2 gr
- Brown sugar 60 gr
- (or white sugar)
- All-purpose flour 35 gr
- Matcha powder 10 gr
- Baking powder 1 gr
- (baking powder)

Implementation tools
Oven, microwave, egg beater,...

How to make Brownie cookie matcha

1. Melt the chocolate butter mixture
White chocolate is cut into small pieces and put in a glass bowl with 30g of butter and then put in the microwave for 30 seconds.

Take the chocolate and use a spoon to stir the ingredients together.

Pro tip: You can put chocolate and butter in a bowl and cook in a water bath over a pot of hot water.
2. Beat eggs
Place 1 egg, 2g vanilla essence and 60g brown sugar in a bowl and beat with a mixer on medium speed until the mixture comes together and bubbles appear.

3. Mix matcha cake powder

Add the white chocolate and melted butter to the egg mixture and mix well with a spatula.

Sift 10gr matcha powder, 35gr all-purpose flour and 1g baking powder into the chocolate egg mixture and mix well with a whisk.

4. Baking cake

Turn on the oven at 170 degrees Celsius 15 minutes before baking.

Put the cake dough into the icing bag and shape the cake on the baking tray and then put in the oven, bake at 160 degrees Celsius for 10-12 minutes.

5. Finished product

The delicious matcha brownie cookie with a strong green tea flavor with a crispy outside and soft inside is a great dessert.

How to preserve cakes?
Do not move the cake until it is completely cooled.
After baking, wait for the cake to cool completely, then put it in a special plastic bag for food, or put it in a sealed container. Do not store the cake while it is still hot because the cake can create moisture that can quickly spoil the cake.

If the cake is mushy, before using you put the cake in the microwave at medium temperature for about 5-10 minutes, the cake will be crispy ag

Ginger Cinnamon Cookies

Ingredients for Ginger Cinnamon Cookies

- All-purpose flour 350 gr
- Cinnamon powder 5 gr
- Ginger powder 10 gr
- Unsalted butter 130 gr
- (to soften)
- Baking soda 5 gr
- (baking salt)
- 1 chicken egg
- Corn syrup 60 ml
- Brown sugar 170 gr

Implementation tools
Oven, bowl, mixer, sieve, cutter mold, rolling pin,...

How to make Ginger Cinnamon Cookies

1.Mix cake dough
First, sift into the bowl 350g flour, 5g baking soda, 5g cinnamon powder, 10g ginger powder and mix well.

Next, add 130g of unsalted butter to soften, mix well by hand until the ingredients are blended, the mixture is loose, discrete and not sticky.

Next, add 170g of brown sugar and continue to mix well.

Small tip: Depending on the absorbency of the flour, you can increase or decrease the amount of corn syrup you need to add. You should add a little corn syrup to avoid the dough being too dry or too mushy.

2. Kneading the dough

Knead the dough with your hands for about 5-7 minutes until the dough forms a uniform mass, not sticky to your hands, neither dry nor pasty.

Next, seal the dough with a plastic bag or food wrap, put it in the refrigerator for about 20 minutes.

Note: You should not over knead the dough because it will make the dough tough.

3. Shape the cake

Put the dough on the table, cover with parchment paper and use a rolling pin. Then, use the mold to press on the dough to shape.

Place the cake on a baking tray lined with parchment paper, then place the cake tray in the refrigerator for 15 minutes before baking.

Outward remittance:

When baking, the cake will rise higher, so you should not roll the dough thick because it will make the cake hard.

If you have time, you should leave the cake in the refrigerator for 12-24 hours, this way will help the cake when baked, it will have a beautiful color and taste better.

4. Baking cake

Preheat the oven at 180 degrees Celsius for 15 minutes, then bake the cake in the middle groove, 2 fire mode at 180 degrees Celsius for 15 - 17 minutes.

5. Finished product

After finished, the biscuits have a slight aroma of ginger and cinnamon, when eaten, they have a moderate crunch, soft and melt in the mouth with a sweet and fatty taste that is mixed with a little warmth from ginger and cinnamon, both delicious and good for health.

Cheese Seaweed Cookies

Ingredients for making Cheese Seaweed Cookies

- Salty biscuits 30 pieces
- (or less sweet)
- Dried seaweed 1 leaf
- Unsalted Butter 50 gr
- Marshmallow 110 gr
- Cheese powder 20 gr
- A2 whole milk powder 10 gr

How to choose and buy fresh ingredients
What is Marshmallow? Where do you buy it?

Marshmallow is a sweet and fluffy marshmallow that is as soft as cotton wool. Unlike other sweets, marshmallows get their sweetness from sucrose (also known as cane sugar). Marshmallow is used as an ingredient for drinks and cakes. The use of marshmallow is to create softness, as well as decorate your cake to become more attractive.
You can easily find marshmallows at supermarkets, bakeries, or order them on e-commerce sites.
What is whole milk powder? Where do you buy it?

Whole milk powder is a type of milk in powder form, which is separated from the pure fresh milk that has been approved for bacteria. Whole milk powder is a fairly common ingredient in baking.

Compared with whole milk, whole milk powder has lower nutritional content but the shelf life is longer (about 6-9 months).

Implementation tools
Oven, non-stick pan, whisk, bowl, spoon,...

How to make Cheese Seaweed Biscuits
1. Sprinkle seaweed on the cake
First, melt 20g of unsalted butter over medium heat for 5 minutes, then spread the butter over the cookies.

Next, use scissors to cut the dried seaweed leaves, sprinkle on the buttered cake, then spread a thin layer of butter.

2. Drying the cake
After you have sprinkled seaweed on the cake, put the cake in the oven to dry for 7-10 minutes at a temperature of 110 degrees Celsius.

3. Cooking the filling
You put the remaining butter in the pan to melt for about 5 minutes, then add 110g of marshmallow and melt for another 5 minutes, then add 10g of A2 whole milk powder and 20g of cheese powder, stir well, then turn off the heat.

Small tip: To enhance the flavor of the cake, you can add seaweed!

4. Multiply

After you have the cake filling, take the cake out of the oven and put the cheese filling in the center of the cake, then take another cake to sandwich it.

You can leave more or less according to your preferences.

5. Finished product

Seaweed biscuits filled with cheese have a faint aroma, the cake has a very beautiful shiny golden color. The biscuit part is crispy, the filling is medium sweet and fatty.

Almond Cookies Cereal

Ingredients to make Almond Cookies Cereal

Cereal 100 gr
100 gr . sliced almonds
Almond flour 100 gr
Material figure
Food ingredients 2 ways to make cereal cookies

Implementation tools
Oven, bowl, knife, parchment paper, spatula

How to make Cereal Almond Cookies

1.Mix the dough
Place in a bowl 100g of sliced almonds and 100g of cereal. Mix well by hand and gently squeeze to break apart the cereal.

Put 100g of almond flour in a bowl of cereal and mix well. Then spread the batter evenly onto a baking tray lined with parchment paper.

2.Baking cake
Preheat oven to 180 degrees C for about 10 minutes. Place the cake tray in the oven and bake for about 20 minutes until the cake is firm.

3.Complete

After baking is complete, you cut the cake into squares to eat while the cake is still hot. Let the cake cool and then you can use it.

4.Finished product

The cake when finished baking will have a beautiful golden brown color with an attractive aroma of almonds. The piece of cake is crispy and delicious, when used with a little tea, it will be very delicious!

Cereal Cookies

Ingredients for Cereal Cookies

- Cereal 50 gr
- All-purpose flour 90 gr
- Corn starch 125 gr

- Milk powder 15 gr
- Powdered sugar 50 gr
- Unsalted Butter 125 gr

Where to buy unsalted butter and powdered milk?
Unsalted butter and milk powder can be purchased at bakeries specializing in baking ingredients, at supermarkets or e-commerce sites.

Implementation tools
Egg beater, oven, sieve, flat spatula, stencils, zip bag,...

How to make Cereal Cookies

1.Grain crumbs
Put 50g of cereal in a zip or plastic bag, fold the bag tightly, roll it into crumbs and put it in a bowl.

2.Mix the dough
Put 125g of unsalted butter in a bowl with 50g of powdered sugar, turn on the mixer at medium speed and beat until the mixture is fluffy.

Using a sieve, sprinkle in 90g of all-purpose flour, 125g of cornstarch, 15g of powdered milk and mix well with a spatula until the dough is mixed together.

Small tip: If you filter the flour through a sieve, it will help the dough to be loose and not clump when mixing.

3. Shape the cookie
Divide the dough into 16g balls and roll them over the rolled cereal bowl.

Place the dough balls on a baking tray lined with parchment paper, then gently press them down with your hands to flatten them. Do the same with the rest of the dough.

4.Baking cake
Preheat oven to 160 degrees Celsius for 10 minutes. Put the cake tray in the oven at 160 degrees Celsius for about 20 minutes until the cake is fragrant and golden.

5.Finished product
Crispy, spongy cereal biscuits with an eye-catching golden color. The crispy outer grain crust helps create a highlight for the cake, when biting into it, you will taste the attractive and fatty flavor of flour and milk, which can make you fall in love with one bite immediately.

Banana Peanut Butter Cookies

Ingredients to prepare for how to make peanut butter banana cookies

- 250g all-purpose flour
- 1 tsp baking powder
- 1/2 tsp cornstarch (corn)
- 1/2 tsp salt
- 1/4 tsp baking soda
- 1/4 tsp cinnamon powder
- 100g soft unsalted butter
- 100g brown sugar
- 1 chicken egg

1 medium-sized banana, peeled and grated
1 tsp vanilla essence
Tools for making peanut butter banana biscuits

Baking tools: Oven, baking tray, parchment paper, whisk, mixing bowl, spatula.

How to make simple peanut butter banana biscuits
Preheat the oven to 180 degrees Celsius. Line a baking sheet with parchment paper to prepare the baking tray before adding the dough.

Place flour ingredients, baking powder, cornstarch (corn), salt, baking soda, and cinnamon in a large bowl.

Then use a mixer to beat the butter with brown sugar at medium-high speed for about 1 to 2 minutes or until the butter is fluffy and pale, add peanut butter, eggs, bananas. Add vanilla and beat on medium-high speed until all ingredients are incorporated, scrape the sides of the bowl with a spatula, then fold the dry flour mixture you mixed in the previous step into the medium butter mixture. continue to grind, grind until the mixture has thickened and the machine can no longer beat, then stop.

Scoop out equal-weight scoops of dough and roll the dough into balls, then spread the balls evenly all over a baking tray lined with parchment paper, ready to move on to the next step of cookie making. banana butter.

Next, use a steel fruit fork that is quite hard and heavy, press firmly but slowly to flatten the dough, you can sprinkle a little raw sugar on top of the cake if you want.

Raw sugar when baked will be very crispy, increasing the attractiveness of the cake, don't worry that the baking sugar will burn. Because we bake the cake in a dry form without generating water, the sugar will not melt or burn.

As in the first step, before mixing the dough, we have prepared an oven with appropriate heat. When it comes to baking, simply place the tray in the oven and bake for about 8 to 10 minutes or until the edges are slightly golden.

Raspberry Jam Cookies

Materail

- Raspberry jam 100 Gr
- Wheat flour 120 Gr
- White Sugar 80 Gr
- Chicken 1 Egg
- Avocado115 Gr
- Corn Flour 80 Gr

IMPLEMENTATION GUIDE

1. Put butter, sugar in a bowl, beat until butter turns light, add egg yolks, beat well.

Put butter, sugar in a bowl, beat until butter turns light, add egg yolks, beat well.
2. Use a whisk to mix the flour and cornstarch, then, pour into a bowl, use a whisk to beat on low to form a smooth mass.

Use a spatula to mix the flour and cornstarch, then, pour into the bowl, beat with a mixer on low to form a smooth mass.
Use a spatula to mix the flour and cornstarch, then, pour into the bowl, beat with a mixer on low to form a smooth mass.
3. Prepare a tray lined with parchment paper, roll the dough into round balls, use a plastic spoon to press flat into the center of the cake as shown below.

Prepare a tray lined with parchment paper, roll the dough into round balls, use a plastic spoon to press flat into the center of the cake as shown below.
4. Bake the cake at 180 degrees C for 15 minutes or until the cake is golden. When the cake cools, place the raspberry jam in the center of the cake hole.

Bake the cake at 180 degrees C for 15 minutes or until the cake is golden. When the cake cools, place the raspberry jam in the center of the cake hole.
5. The result is done, wish you all success and deliciousness with this cake!

Apple Cookies

Prepare the ingredients

- 1 apple, diced
- 120g unsalted butter
- 100g flour
- 130g sugar
- 130g oatmeal

- 1 egg
- 13g cinnamon powder
- 1.3g nutmeg
- 1.3g baking soda
- 65g dried blueberries
- 5ml vanilla extract or 5g vanilla powder
- 1 pinch of salt

How to make

Step 1: Put the butter and sugar in a clean bowl and beat with a spoon to form a light yellow mixture.

Step 2: Continue to put in the bowl of butter and sugar 1 teaspoon of vanilla and 1 egg, beat well to form a smooth, thick paste.

Step 3: Put the ingredients: flour, 130g oats, 13g cinnamon powder, 1 tablespoon baking soda in another clean, dry bowl and mix well.

Step 4: Sift the flour mixture in step 3 into the butter and egg mixture above. Then, use a spatula to mix the flour evenly.

Step 5: Apples are washed, peeled and then cut into small dices. Chopped almonds. Add the apple and chopped almond mixture to the flour mixture in step 4 and mix well.

Step 6: Add blueberries to the mixture to enhance the taste (if you don't have blueberries, you can skip this step). Line a baking tray with parchment paper and then use a spoon to scoop the mixture into the tray. Put the tray in the oven at 150 degrees C for about 15 minutes, the cake is cooked.

Step 6: Take the cake out of the mold, let it cool, then put it in an airtight container and use it once.

Notes:

How to make apple biscuits is not too complicated, but in the process, you need to keep a few things in mind for the best results:

Baking mold should choose the type made from alloy material. Before baking, line the bottom of the pan with parchment paper to make it easier to remove the cake. During the baking process, it is recommended to cut a number of holes on the surface of the cake so that the heat is evenly distributed so that the cake cooks quickly and does not crack after baking.
Should choose the type of apple stone apple pie will be more delicious because this apple has a firm, sweet and very fragrant pulp.

Almond Green Tea Cookies

Ingredients for Almond Green Tea Cookies

- All-puMatcha powder 1 tbsp
- Unsalted Butter 113 gr
- Almonds 1 tbsp
- Sugar 100 gr
- Salt 1/4 teaspoon
- flour 135 gr

Where to buy sliced almonds?
Sliced almonds you can easily find and buy at nut stores, bakeries or large supermarkets.
You should choose packages of carefully packaged almonds, pay attention to the expiration date and consider the quality of the nuts. If the almond slices are ivory white, whole, and not moldy or broken, you can buy them.
Besides, you can use whole almonds and then crumble them into cakes, which is also very delicious.
See also: Health benefits of almonds
Food ingredients 2 ways to make Japanese green tea cookies - green tea cookies

Implementation tools
Oven, bowl, mixer, knife, stencils,...

How to make Almond Green Tea Cookies
1.Mix matcha green tea powder
First, sift into a bowl 135g flour, 1/4 teaspoon salt, 1 tablespoon matcha powder and mix well.

2.Mix the flour mixture with the almond butter
Next, mash 113g of unsalted butter with 100g of sugar. Then, slowly add the green tea powder mixture to the butter bowl and continue to mix.

Next, add 1 tablespoon of sliced almonds and mix one more time so that the ingredients in the batter are evenly mixed.

3. Kneading and shaping
Roll the dough out by hand and put it in the freezer for 15 minutes to harden the dough, making it easier to cut and shape cookies.

After 30 minutes, cut the cake into bite-sized pieces about half a finger thick.

4.Baking cake
Preheat oven to 160 degrees Celsius for 10 minutes.

After 10 minutes, put the cake in the oven, bake at 160 degrees C for 15 minutes. Then you take the cake out, let it cool and enjoy immediately.

5.Finished product
The almond green tea biscuits that have just come out of the oven are fragrant with butter, the bite is crispy, but it melts in the mouth, especially the aroma and mild bitterness characteristic of matcha powder and crispy almonds. This cake is so simple yet so delicious!

Eggless Soybean Cookies

Ingredients for making Eggless Soybean Cookies

- Soybean meal 40 gr
- Pastry Flour 200 gr
- Soy milk 55 gr
- Cane sugar 70 gr
- Cooking oil 55 gr
- 1 little baking powder

Implementation tools
Oven, bowl, mixer, stencils, knife,...

How to make Eggless Soybean Cookies

1.Mix cake dough
Put in a bowl 55g cooking oil, 70g cane sugar, 55g soy milk and stir well to blend.

Next, sift into the bowl 200g flour, 40g soybean flour, 1 little baking soda and mix well until the dough is sticky.

2. Knead the dough and shape the cake
Knead the dough with your hands for 10 minutes until the dough is smooth.

Then, roll the dough into a long cylinder, wrap it in parchment paper, and put it in the refrigerator for 30 minutes.

After 30 minutes, use a knife to cut the cake into slices about 1/2 inch thick.

3.Baking cake
Preheat the oven to 180 degrees Celsius for 15 minutes, then bake the cake for 15 minutes at 180 degrees Celsius.

4. Finished product

Biscuits have a soft, spongy texture that melts in the mouth, with a light sweetness and a characteristic aroma from soybeans, both delicious and nutritious.

Tips for preserving cakes

Let the cake cool completely, place in an airtight bag or container and store in a cool place for 1 month.
You can add more grains to add more flavor to the cake.
Cake can be used for vegans.

Peach Cookies

Ingredients for Peach Cookies

- Unsalted Butter 80 gr
- Sugar 140 gr

- All-purpose flour 370 gr
- (wheat flour number 11)
- Chicken eggs 2
- Lemon juice 10 ml
- Vanilla essence 5 ml
- Chocolate 100 gr
- Peach syrup 2 teaspoons
- Whipping cream 50 ml
- 1 little pink food coloring
- 1 little yellow food coloring
- Filtered water 100 ml

Implementation tools
Oven, bowl, mixer, cup,...

How to make Peach Cookies

1.Mix cake dough
Puree 80g unsalted butter, then add 140g sugar and stir until the sugar dissolves, the mixture is no longer lumpy.

Next, add 370gr of finely sifted flour, 2 eggs, 10ml of lemon juice, 5ml of vanilla essence. Use your hands to mix the dough until it forms a smooth, non-sticky ball.

Finally, cover the dough and let it rest for about 30 minutes.

2.Shaping the cake
Divide the dough into equal parts, about 20g each, and then roll into balls.

Then, you put the dough into the mold lined with parchment paper.

3.Baking cake
Preheat the oven to 170 degrees Celsius for 10 minutes, then bake the cakes for 15 minutes at 170 degrees Celsius.

Once the cake is done, leave it out to cool completely.

4.Make Chocolate Sauce
In a bowl, add 100g of chopped chocolate, 50ml of whipping cream, and heat in a water bath until melted. Use a spatula to stir until the chocolate mixture is combined.

When the chocolate cools, place it in a piping bag.

5.Peach shape
Use a round mold or an ice cream catcher to drill a round hole in the bottom of the cake. Then, you pump the chocolate sauce inside.

Next, turn the 2 chocolate-filled cake parts together for adhesion.

Tinting:

Prepare 2 cups containing about 50ml of filtered water, add 1 teaspoon of peach syrup to each cup.

Then, you mix in each cup a little yellow and pink food coloring and stir well.

Roll 1/2 of the cake in a cup of yellow water and then roll the other half in a cup of pink water.

Finally, coat the cake evenly through a layer of sugar and it's done.

6.Finished product
Biscuits have eye-catching colors, crunchy, soft and melt in the mouth with the sweet taste of butter and sugar and a slight bitterness from chocolate.

How to preserve cakes?
Put the cake in an airtight container, store it in the refrigerator and use it for 2-3 days to keep the deliciousness of the cake!

Cherry Blossom Cookies

Ingredients for Cherry Blossom Cookies

- All-purpose flour 125 gr
- Unsalted Butter 90 gr
- Egg yolk 1 pc
- 15 pcs cherry blossom petals
- Powdered sugar 50 gr
- Vanilla essence 1/2 teaspoon

Where to buy salted cherry blossoms?
You can find salted cherry blossoms at Japanese ingredient stores, bakeries, or buy them online on e-commerce sites.

Implementation tools
Egg beater, oven, sieve, flower-shaped cake cutter, stencils (baking paper), rolling pin,...

How to make Cherry Blossom Cookies

1.Mix the dough
Before mixing the powder, soak the salted cherry blossoms in water for 30 minutes to soften them. Then, take out the cherry blossoms and put them on a paper towel to absorb the water.

Use an electric mixer to beat 90g of unsalted butter at room temperature, then sift in 50g of powdered sugar and beat until well combined.

After the butter sugar has melted, add 1 egg yolk and 1/2 teaspoon of vanilla essence and continue to use a whisk to beat together.

After beating, you divide 125g of flour into 2 and then continue to sift the flour into the mixed mixture, then use a mixer to mix well.

Finally, you use a flat spatula to mix again to make the dough more even.

2.Shaping the cake
When the dough is even, put the dough on parchment paper (baking paper), use your hands to press the dough thinly and put it in the refrigerator for 15 minutes.

After 15 minutes, take the dough out and use a rolling pin to roll the dough to about 5mm thin.

After rolling, you use a flower-shaped mold to cut into the dough to shape.

Next, put the dough back in the refrigerator for 15 minutes.

3.Baking cake

After 15 minutes, take out the dough and separate each piece of dough that has been pressed into the shape of a flower, spread it out on a baking tray lined with parchment paper, and place salted cherry blossoms on each piece of dough.

Next, bake the cake at 170 degrees Celsius for 18 - 20 minutes.

Pro tip: For the oven to stabilize, remember to preheat the oven 15 - 30 minutes before baking.
When the cake is done, take it out to cool and enjoy.

4.Finished product
So we have finished the extremely delicious salted cherry blossom biscuits. The cookie is extremely beautiful because it has cherry blossoms as the highlight, plus the aroma from the butter makes the cake more attractive.

Cashew Cookies

Ingredients for Cashew Cookies

- Wheat flour number 13 300 gr
- Cashew nuts 200 gr
- Cashew nuts 30 seeds
- Butter 200 gr

- Baking powder 1 tbsp
- 100 gr. milled sugar
- Cinnamon powder 1 tbsp
- 1 chicken egg

Implementation tools
Oven, whisk, mixer

How to make Cashew Cookies

1. Finely grind cashews
Put 200g of cashews into a blender and puree it.

2. Mix cake dough
In a bowl, add 300g of flour 13, ground cashews, 1 tablespoon of baking powder, 1 tablespoon of cinnamon powder and mix well.

3. Melt butter
In a new bowl, 200g butter, 100g sugar, mix with a whisk until the mixture is smooth.

Add 1 egg and continue to mix.

Pro tip: You can mash the butter and mix it with a spoon.
4. Mix the dough with butter
Place the cake batter in the butter bowl and mix until well combined.

5. Shape the cake
Take a little dough ball, press it slightly flat and then place the cashews on top.

6. Baking cake
Preheat the oven to 150 degrees Celsius for 10 minutes, then put the cake in the oven for 20 minutes.

7. Finished product
When finished, the biscuits are crispy, fragrant and sweet with a little bit of flesh and fat from delicious fresh cashews.

Orange Cookies

Ingredients for Orange Cookies

- 2 oranges
- Unsalted Butter 75 gr
- Powdered sugar 60 gr

- Salt 1 teaspoon
- 1 egg
- Vanilla extract 2 gr
- Household flour 140 gr
- Almond powder 20 gr
- Baking powder 1 gr
- Orange peel 10 gr

How to make Fresh Orange Biscuits

1.Mix egg butter mixture
75g unsalted butter you keep at room temperature, put in a bowl and mash.. Then add 60g sugar and 1/2 teaspoon salt and mix well, add eggs and vanilla extract, add orange peel.

2.Mix cake dough
Next, sift 140g flour, 25g almond flour and 1g baking powder. Stir the mixture until the ingredients come together into a thick and pliable mixture.

3.Rolling the dough
Use a rolling pin to flatten the dough, then use a round mold to shape the cake. Place the cake on a baking sheet lined with parchment paper.

4.Cut oranges
Oranges are washed, peeled and cut into thin slices.

Next you put the orange pieces on the cake dough, sprinkle some almond powder on the cake.

5. Baking cake

Put the cake in the microwave and bake it twice on the lowest temperature for 9 minutes each time. After baking, you let the cake cool completely, the cake will be more crispy than when hot.

6. Finished product

Orange biscuits are sweet, delicious, and melt in the mouth. The special flavor of biscuits has a characteristic mild orange flavor that stimulates the taste buds to eat more deliciously without being bored.

How to choose to buy delicious fresh oranges

Should choose the big round fruit, thin skin, bright yellow color, lots of essential oil. Because these will be delicious oranges, with a lot of water and sweetness.

You choose oranges with uniform yellow color, thin skin and glossy skin, which are always succulent.

When choosing, you should choose firm fruits, while soft and spongy ones are prone to waterlogging.

With this cake, you should choose American yellow oranges (American Navel yellow oranges) with sweet, succulent, light aroma to make the cake more delicious.

How to store orange biscuits

Do not move the cake until it is completely cooled.

After baking, wait for the cake to cool completely, then put it in a special plastic bag for food, or put it in a sealed container. Do not store the cake while it is still hot because it can create moisture that can cause the cake to spoil quickly. If the cake is mushy, before using you put the cake in the microwave at medium temperature for about 5-10 minutes, the cake will be crispy again.

Keto Lemon Cookies

Ingredients for Keto Lemon Cookies

- Salted Butter 70 gr
- Sugar 4 teaspoons
- (diet sugar)
- 1 egg
- Almond powder 120 gr
- Coconut flour 60 gr
- Baking powder 1 teaspoon
- (baking soda)
- Lemon juice 2 tbsp
- Lemon peel 1 teaspoon
- (finely grated)
- Material figure
- Ingredients for Keto Lemon Cookies

Implementation tools
Oven, stirrer, bowl,...

How to make Keto Lemon Cookies

1. Melt butter
Put in a bowl 70g salted butter and 4 teaspoons of sugar, then use a spatula to mash the butter.

Continue to add 1 egg and beat the mixture well.

Outward remittance:

You can replace diet sugar with stevia, xylitol, sucralose, aspartame, ... depending on the type of sugar, the sweetness is different, so it can be adjusted compared to the recipe.

2. Mix cake dough

Add 120g of almond flour, 60g of coconut flour and 1 teaspoon of baking soda to the butter mixture, then use a spatula to stir the mixture.

Add 2 tablespoons of lemon juice to the batter and stir well.

3. Shape the cake

Divide the dough into small balls, shape the dough with your hands and place on a tray lined with parchment paper.

Use a fork to shape the cake.

4. Finished product

Put some lemon zest on top of the cake and that's it, delicious keto lemon cookies are complete. Each piece of cake is crispy with the fragrant aroma of almond flour, coconut flour and the aromatic sourness of lemon when used with a cup of tea is much better.

How to store cakes:

Do not put the cake in a plastic bag to preserve it while the cake is still warm, the cake may create steam, when wrapped, it will easily make the cake moldy and quickly damaged. Wait for the cake to cool completely and cover it with plastic wrap (specialized in food wrap), seal tightly, do not let air in.
After wrapping, you should store the cake in a cool and dry place in the room. If the temperature is too hot, you can put it in the refrigerator.

Sweet Potato Cookies

Ingredients for Sweet Potato Cookies

- Steamed sweet potato 125 gr
- Glutinous rice flour 90 gr
- Fresh milk 40 ml
- Sugar 20 gr
- Honey 30 gr

How to choose delicious sweet potatoes, not shy
Buy sweet potatoes with a healthy appearance, not cracked, chipped. Picking up the potato feels heavy, hard, not crushed.
Be careful when you see that the potatoes are black or pitted, which is a sign that the sweet potatoes are spoiled.
Choose potatoes with a round or elongated shape, no waist, hollow, lightly squeezed, not too hard, these tubers are usually less fibrous, have a lot of flour and are very sweet to eat.
You should not choose tubers that are too small, long, waisted or hollow because there will be a lot of fiber.

Implementation tools
Oven, bowl, mixer, cup, steamer,...

How to make Sweet Potato Cookies

1.Mashed sweet potato
Put in a bowl of 125g steamed sweet potatoes and mash them with a fork.

2.Mix cake dough
Add to the bowl of potatoes 40ml fresh milk, 20g sugar, 30g honey, 90g glutinous flour.

Use a spatula to mix until the dough forms a smooth dough.

3. Shape the cake
Divide the dough into portions and roll them into balls.

Next, use your hands to slightly flatten the dough and then use a toothpick to press on the surface to create stripes.

4.Baking cake
Preheat the oven to 180 degrees Celsius for 10 minutes, then put the cake into the oven for 15 minutes at 180 degrees Celsius.

5.Finished product
The biscuits have a soft and spongy outer shell, the inside is chewy from glutinous rice flour, sweet potato flavor, extremely easy to eat.

Corn Cookies

Ingredients for Corn Cookies

- Unsalted Butter 110 gr
- Sugar 120 gr
- Eggs 30 gr

- Cake dough 83 gr
- Cornmeal 57 gr
- Baking powder 2 gr
- Baking soda 1 gr
- Salt 1/3 teaspoon
- Corn kernels 35 gr
- Implementation tools:
- Oven, egg beater

How to make Corn Cookies - Corn Cookies

1. Beat butter with sugar
Put in a bowl of 110g unsalted butter, beat until melted at high speed for 1 minute until soft.

Add 120g sugar, and beat until sugar dissolves. Beat until the mixture is fluffy and light in color.

Beat the mixture for about 3 minutes 45 seconds, depending on the machine.

Small tips:

Unsalted butter you should cut into small pieces to beat with sugar faster and more evenly.
The butter needs to be softened at room temperature but not to the point of mushy or watery.

Make sure you beat the butter thoroughly because the cake swells and is spongy thanks to the air bubbles in the whipped butter.

2. Beat the egg butter mixture

Stir in 1 egg. Add the eggs to the butter bowl above and continue to mix at high speed until well combined.

Total mixing time is about 2 minutes 45 seconds.

3Mix the cake batter

Sift into a bowl 83g cake flour, 57g cornstarch, 2g baking powder, 1g baking soda, 1/3 teaspoon salt.

Mix the flour mixture well. Put 35g corn kernels in a bowl, mix well.

Note:

You just mix the flour until the flour blends with the butter into a block, then stop, do not mix the dough too thoroughly, the cake will be disjointed.

If the dough is too wet, it may be because your butter is too soft, or if you do it for a long time, the butter will melt, or it may be because the flour used has poor water absorption. You fix it by adding dry flour slowly (or put the dough in the fridge to harden the butter).

The dough is too dry and sticky, maybe because you use too much flour, leading to the dough not having enough cohesion. You can fix it by adding little by little cooking oil and mixing until the mixture is satisfactory.

4.Baking cake

Use an ice cream scoop or a regular spoon to create a round shape for the cake dough ball as shown.

Put the dough into the cake tray (lined with parchment paper to prevent sticking).

Preheat the oven at 175 degrees Celsius for 15 minutes to stabilize the oven temperature.

Put the cake tray in the oven and bake the cake at 175 degrees C for 12 - 15 minutes.

When the cake is done baking, let the cake cool and harden, then move the cake to the rack (rack) and let it cool completely. So the cookie worked.

Tip: You should arrange the cakes a little apart so that the cakes after baking, expand and do not stick together.

5.Finished product

Corn Cookies - Delicious sponge corn biscuits with fragrant, fatty and sweet taste of corn are really attractive, aren't they? Let's go to the kitchen to make it right now!

Tips for successful implementation

Each type of oven has a different baking temperature difference. You can fix it to bake better by using an oven thermometer or by monitoring the cake regularly to adjust the temperature, baking time and baking groove accordingly.
Do not put the cake in a plastic bag to preserve it while the cake is still warm, the cake may create steam, when wrapped, it will easily make the cake moldy and quickly damaged. Wait for the cake to cool completely and cover it with plastic wrap (specialized in food wrap), seal tightly, do not let air in.

After wrapping, you should store the cake in a cool and dry place in the room. If the temperature is too hot, you can put it in the refrigerator.

Cheese Cookies

Ingredients for Cheese Cookies

- All-purpose flour 100 g
- Cheese powder 40 g
- Salt 1/4 teaspoon
- Unsalted Butter 50 g
- Powdered sugar 30 g
- Egg yolk 1 pc

Implementation tools
bowl, stirrup, oven,...

How to make Cheese Biscuits

1.Mix cake dough
Sift into the bowl 100g flour, 40g cheese powder, 1/4 teaspoon salt, then use a spatula to mix.

2. Beat the egg butter mixture
Put in a bowl 50g soft unsalted butter (but not runny), 30g powdered sugar, 1 teaspoon vanilla, 1 egg yolk and stir with a whisk.

3.Mix flour with egg butter mixture
Add the cake batter to the butter and egg mixture and use a spatula to mix until the dough forms a ball.

Cover the dough with cling film and place in the fridge for 30 minutes.

Small tip: Remember to divide the dough into 2 parts and then mix each part in turn, so the mixture will be more blended.

4. Shape the cake
Cover the dough with a layer of parchment paper, roll the dough thinly with a stick, then use a chopstick to poke many holes in the surface to shape.

Cut the dough into triangles, cover with parchment paper and place in the fridge for 15 minutes.

5.Baking cake
Preheat the oven for 10 minutes at 160 degrees Celsius.

Place the cake in the middle of the oven and bake at 160 degrees Celsius for 15 minutes.

6.Finished product
When finished, the biscuits will be spongy, crispy and fragrant with greasy cheese.

Almond Chocolate Keto Cookies

Ingredients for Almond Chocolate Keto Cookies

- Almond powder 100 grams
- Almonds 100 grams
- Honey 120 grams
- Cocoa powder 160 grams
- Unsalted butter 55 grams
- (Can replace Tuong An butter)
- 2 eggs
- Baking powder 1 teaspoon

Implementation tools
Oven, sieve, micro scale

How to make Chocolate Almond Keto Cookies

1.Mix the dough
First, sift 100g of almond powder, 160g of cocoa powder and 1 teaspoon of baking powder into a large bowl. If you only have almonds, you can finely grind them to make a regular flour.

Next, you add in the bowl 120g of honey, 2 eggs and then use a whisk to mix the mixture. At this point the dough is quite dry and loose.

Then you cut the seeds and put them in the flour bowl and then add 55g of melted butter (boiled in a water bath) to the bowl. Then use a spatula to mix the mixture into a smooth dough.

Tip:

You can increase or decrease the amount of honey or replace honey with sugar. In addition, you can also add chocolate chips to enhance the flavor of the cake.
If you have a whisk, use it to save time as well as help the dough more evenly.

2.Shaping the cake

After the dough is mixed, continue to squeeze the dough into balls like balls and then put them on a baking tray lined with parchment paper.

Then you use your hands to flatten the cake and decorate the top with different nuts.

Tip: You can also shape the cake into different shapes depending on each person's preference. However, do not let the cake layer be too thick because the baking time will be long, the cake will be difficult to cook and soft.

3.Baking cake

Preheat oven to 180 degrees Celsius for 7-10 minutes. Preheating the oven will help keep the baking temperature more stable.

After preheating the oven, put the cake in the oven in the middle of the oven and bake at 180 degrees Celsius for 15 minutes.

Note: Depending on the type of oven, the temperature difference is different, so during the baking process you need to regularly monitor the cake to avoid burning the cake.

4.Finished product
Chocolate almond keto cookies not only taste delicious but also help you lose weight well. With a simple and extremely easy recipe, this is probably the cake you should try and don't miss it.

Tips to preserve cakes for a long time

After the cake is done baking, let it cool down and then put it in an airtight container and keep it in a well-ventilated place. You can also store the cake in the refrigerator to eat later.

Chocolate Cookies

Ingredients for Chocolate Cookies

- Wheat flour number 11 300 gr
- Powdered sugar 150 gr
- Salt 1 gr
- Sprouts 2.5 gr
- (baking soda)
- Cocoa powder 10 gr
- Unsalted Butter 185 gr
- Chicken eggs 2
- (yolk - chilled)
- Chocolate chips 100 gr

Implementation tools
Air fryer, air fryer, bowl...

How to make Chocolate Cookies

1.Mix the dough
Put 300g flour, 150g powdered sugar, 1g salt, 2.5g baking soda in a bowl. You should sift the ingredients through a sieve to make the dough smooth, the cake after making will be more delicious.

Add 10g of sifted cocoa powder to the flour mixture and mix well.

Mash 185g softened butter, add 2 egg yolks, 7.5ml vanilla and stir well.

Divide the dough into portions and add little by little to the butter mixture, mixing with a spatula. Then, use your hands to knead several times until the dough forms a ball, the dough is not too dry.

Add 100g of chocolate chips to the flour mixture, mix again and you're done.

2.Shaping
Shape the dough into round balls, you can shape it to a large or small size depending on your preference. Continue to use your hands to gently press down to flatten the cake.

Then sprinkle some chocolate chips on the cake to decorate.

3.Baking cake
Preheat the air fryer before baking for about 15 minutes at 160 degrees Celsius.

Place the cake in the air fryer and bake for 15 minutes.

4.Finished product
The cake after baking has a beautiful brown color. When eaten, it is crispy, fragrant with butter, sweet and fatty taste of soola.

Note:

After baking, the cake will still be soft. You should let the cake cool naturally, the cake will be more crispy and spongy.
Do not move the cake until it is completely cooled.

Coffee Bean Cookies

Ingredients for making Coffee Bean Cookies

- All-purpose flour 125 gr
- (or 13th flour)
- Cornstarch 25 gr
- Pure coffee powder 1 teaspoon
- (5 - 7g)
- Cocoa powder 1 tbsp
- (about 12 - 15g)
- Unsalted Butter 75 gr
- Fresh milk 50 ml
- Powdered sugar 55 gr
- Egg yolk 1 pc

How to choose and buy quality ingredients
What is all-purpose flour? Where to buy reputable all-purpose flour

All-purpose flour (or wheat flour number 11) is a flour with a high protein content of about 11.5 - 12% and is often used to make chewy cakes such as bread, pillow cakes or pizza. The high amount of protein in the dough will combine well with the yeast to create the chewiness of the finished cake.
What is cocoa powder? Where to buy cocoa powder?

Cocoa powder is a powder produced from the seeds of the cocoa fruit. The powder is dark brown in color, passionate aroma, bitter taste, fleshy.

There are two types of cocoa powder on the market: ready-made and pure. Depending on the preferences and purposes of use, users can optionally choose the right powder for themselves.

Implementation tools
Oven, sieve, bowl, cup, knife,...

How to make Coffee Bean Cookies
1.Prepare the butter and coffee mixture
First, you dissolve 1 teaspoon of pure coffee powder with 50ml of hot fresh milk.

Then, you put in a new bowl: 75g unsalted butter, 55g powdered sugar and stir until the sugar dissolves and the mixture is smooth. Next, add 1 egg yolk, coffee mixture and mix again.

2.Prepare the cookie dough
Next, you sift into the bowl of butter: 125g flour, 25g cornstarch, 1 tablespoon cocoa powder and mix well to bind the ingredients.

At this time, use your hands to knead the dough for about 3-5 minutes until it forms a smooth, non-sticky mass. Then, cover the dough and let it rest for 30 minutes.

3.Shaping coffee beans for cakes
Divide the dough into small balls of about 6 - 8g / 1 tablet, then use your hands to shape into an oval shape.

Next, use a knife to press the center of the cake into the shape of a coffee bean. In order for the cake to keep its shape after baking, when finished shaping, put the cake in the refrigerator for 20 minutes.

4..Baking cookies
Pre-heat the oven to 150 degrees for 10 minutes to preheat the oven.

After 10 minutes, put the cake in the oven on the middle tray and bake at 165 - 170 degrees C for 20 - 25 minutes depending on whether you like it medium or crispy.

5.Finished product
Coffee bean biscuits are small, lovely and fragrant, try a bite of crispy, sweet, fatty and a little bitter, very tasty.

What's better than using cake with some fresh milk or coffee?

Tips for successful implementation
Using pure cocoa powder without sugar will make the cake taste better, do not use milk cocoa or sugary milo powder.

It is recommended to use unsalted butter for the cake to have a fatty aroma and not to use margarine. When done, the butter needs to be softened at room temperature, but not melted.

Do not stack cakes close to each other, because when baked, the cakes will expand and stick together.
Each type of oven has a different baking temperature difference. You can fix it to bake better by using an oven thermometer or by monitoring the cake regularly to adjust the temperature, baking time and baking groove accordingly.

You should make the cake according to the instructions for the delicious crispy cake.
To preserve the cake, you should let it cool completely and store it in an airtight bag or container. In addition, the cake should be stored in a cool, dry place and avoid humid places.

Chocolate Candy Cane Cookies

Ingredients for making Chocolate Candy Cane Cookies

- Candy cane 100 gr
- (spall)
- All-purpose flour 125 gr
- Cocoa powder 60 gr
- Baking soda 3 gr
- Crushed chocolate 170 gr
- (optional type)
- Dark chocolate 120 gr
- (60% cocoa)
- Unsalted Butter 113 gr
- 2 eggs
- Sugar 200 gr
- Salt 3 gr
- 3ml mint essence

Information about ingredients
What is candy cane?

This is a candy shaped like a stick, an image associated with the Christmas season. These candies often have two alternating white and red colors and have a sweet, minty flavor.

Implementation tools
Egg beater, oven, whisk, ice cream scoop, flat spatula, baking tray, stencils (baking paper),...

How to make Chocolate Candy Cane Cookies

1. Melt butter and chocolate
Place 120g of dark chocolate and 113g of unsalted butter in a glass bowl, place in a pot of boiling water, then heat in a water bath over medium heat.

Use a spatula to stir the mixture quickly and evenly. Then take it down and let it cool.

2. Beat eggs
In a bowl, beat 2 eggs with 120g of sugar.

Use an electric mixer to beat the mixture until light froth, many small bubbles appear, then add 3ml of mint extract and melted chocolate mixture. Continue beating the mixture until combined.

3.Mix dry powder
In another bowl, sift 125 grams of flour, 3 grams of baking soda and 3 grams of salt, and then use a whisk to mix well.

4.Mix the cake mix
Add half of the dry powder mixture to the chocolate mixture that has just been beaten in step 2, use a flat spatula to gently mix until the powder dissolves

Continue to add the remaining half of the flour and 60g of cocoa powder, mix well until the flour mixture is combined.

Finally, add 170g of chocolate chips, stir well to finish the cake mixture.

Pro tip: Breaking up the flour mixture makes it easier to mix and the cake mix to homogenize faster.

5.Baking cake
Preheat oven to 165 degrees Celsius before baking for 15-20 minutes.

Use an ice cream scoop to scoop the dough into a tray lined with baking paper, spaced about 5cm apart.

Place candy cane crumbs on the dough balls. Then put the cake tray in the oven and bake at 165 degrees Celsius for 10-15 minutes until the cake is fully baked.

Pro tip: During the baking process, you should use a light-colored (except black) baking tray, which will transfer heat better and help the cake to burn less.

6.Finished product
Once the cake is done, take it out of the oven and let it cool. While the cake is still warm, you can place more candy cane crumbs on top of the cake.

Chocolate candy cane cookies with the aroma of butter, the bitter taste of chocolate and beautiful colors from candy cane are so attractive and unique, aren't they? Let's go to the kitchen and make it right now!

Tips for preserving cookies
After baking, wait for the cake to cool completely, then put it in a special plastic bag for food, or put it in a sealed container. Do not store the cake while it is still hot because it can create moisture that can cause the cake to spoil quickly.
If the cake is mushy, before using you put the cake in the microwave oven at medium temperature for about 5-10 minutes, the cake will be crispy again.

Banana Oatmeal Cookies

Ingredients for Banana Oatmeal Cookie Cookies

- Rolled oats 50 gr
- Rolled oats 50 gr
- 2 soft ripe bananas
- Chia seeds 10 gr
- Pumpkin seeds 10 gr
- Chocolate chips 10 gr
- Cocoa powder 2 teaspoons

How to choose to buy oats to make cookies

You can choose to buy rolled oats or rolled oats to make cakes. When buying oats, you should pay attention to buy oats that are still dry, when gently shaken, the oat pieces come apart, not wet and stick together.

When choosing to buy, you should buy reputable brands that are packed or boxed carefully, you also need to check the expiration date before buying, avoid choosing to buy bags or boxes of oats near the expiration date because they can The circuit is damp and has a strange smell.

How to choose to buy ripe bananas

You should choose to buy ripe green and yellow fruits alternately. These bananas are usually ripened naturally, not chemically pressed.

Naturally ripe bananas, the stem, stem and bunch will ripen evenly (even though there will be green fruit). Ripe bananas will have yellow fruit, but the stem is hard and sometimes green.

Avoid buying bananas that are evenly ripened, beautifully colored, and unusually large. In addition, you should not buy crushed fruits.

What is cocoa powder? Distinguish cocoa powder and chocolate powder

What is cocoa powder?

Cocoa powder is a powder that is ground from the residue of chocolate liquor - a dark brown mixture when finely ground cocoa beans.

Natural cocoa powder cocoa powder is light brown in color, but if it has been processed (alkylated) it will have a darker brown color, which can range from reddish brown to almost black.

In addition to being used as a drink, cocoa powder is also one of the familiar ingredients in baking recipes or drinks.

Distinguish cocoa powder and chocolate powder

The powder is ground from chocolate liquor after being pressed to obtain a liquid, with the cocoa butter removed. And chocolate powder is a mixture of cocoa powder and cocoa butter, mixed with sugar and milk

Natural cocoa powder has a light brown color while chocolate powder consists of 3 types: dark, white and brown chocolate powder

Untreated cocoa powder has a characteristic bitter taste, a slight sour taste, and chocolate powder has a different sweetness and bitterness depending on the milk sugar ratio.

Ingredients for banana oat cookies cookies

Implementation tools
Oven, bowl, spoon, baking tray, stencils,...

How to make Banana Oatmeal Cookies

1. Puree banana
Peel the banana, then put it in a bowl and mash it with a fork.

Small tip: Bananas should be selected for soft ripe fruit but not crushed, it will be easier when mashed and will be sweeter and more fragrant when eaten.

2.Mix the cake flour mixture
In turn, put in a bowl of mashed bananas, a mixture of ingredients including: 50g rolled oats, 50g rolled oats, 10g chia seeds, 10g pumpkin seeds, 10g chocolate chips, 2 teaspoons cocoa powder.

Then you mix all the mixtures in a bowl for about 5 minutes until the dough is thick and sticky.

3. Divide the dough and shape the cake

You divide the dough into equal parts, then wear plastic gloves to prevent the dough from sticking to your hands and ensure hygiene.

Next, you shape each part of the dough into a round ball and then use your hand to flatten it to make the cake into a round shape like a cookie.

4. Baking cake

First, turn on the oven and preheat it to 160 degrees Celsius for 10 minutes.

Next, you line a layer of non-stick paper on the tray and then arrange the cake in turn on the tray and put the cake in the oven.

Adjust the temperature to 160 degrees Celsius and bake for about 15 minutes, then turn the cake over and bake for another 5 minutes, until the cake is cooked, fragrant and the surface is slightly golden.

5. Finished product

Banana Oatmeal Cookies have the brown color of cocoa, when eating you will feel the crunchiness and sweetness of the banana, add a little flavor of oats and especially the crunchy, fleshy taste of pumpkin seeds. very interesting.

Sipping cake with a cup of hot tea for winter day snacks is very suitable.

How to preserve delicious and crispy cookies for a long time:
Put the cake in a sealed bag or box, add a desiccant bag, and then keep it in a ventilated place, away from sunlight and use it up in 2-3 weeks.
Put the cake in an airtight container and bag and then keep it in the refrigerator, this way the cake can be preserved for 4-6 weeks.

Oatmeal Black Sesame Cookies

Ingredients for making Oatmeal Black Sesame Cookies

- Oatmeal 100 gr
- Wheat flour 100 gr
- Black sesame 20 gr
- Olive oil 30 ml
- Honey 20 ml
- Fresh milk 175 ml
- Salt 1/2 teaspoon

How to choose to buy delicious black sesame

You should choose to buy black sesame without dust, dirt, sesame surface looks bright and clean.

Usually, black sesame that has not been treated clean still retains the smell of the soil. Therefore, you should choose sesame with a characteristic aroma to ensure better hygiene and quality!

In addition, you can also buy black sesame that has been packaged with the manufacturer's name on the packaging, clear product details if you find it difficult to do the above two ways.

Where to buy oatmeal?

In addition, you can also choose and order oatmeal at e-commerce site bachhoaxanh.com to save time and travel costs and still buy quality products!

Ingredients for oat black sesame biscuits

Implementation tools
Oil-free fryer, non-stick pan, knife, spoon, stencil,...

How to make Oatmeal Black Sesame Cookies

1.Mix ingredients
First, put a non-stick pan on the stove and roast 20g of black sesame for about 3 minutes until the sesame is just cooked and fragrant.

Pour 100g of oatmeal into 100g of sifted flour in a bowl.

Next, turn 1/2 teaspoon of salt, roasted black sesame into the mixture and stir well.

Slowly pour 175ml milk into the mixture and mix well until the mixture is sticky.

Then, pour 30ml of olive oil, 20ml of honey into the flour mixture and lightly knead for the ingredients to blend together.

Outward remittance:

You should not pour all the milk directly into the powder. Instead, you should base on the quality of the flour to adjust the amount of milk accordingly, avoiding the dough being too mushy or dry.

2.Shaping
Let the dough rest for about 10 minutes. Then, spread the parchment down on a flat surface and place the dough in the center. Fold the parchment paper in half and roll out the dough to about 2mm thick.

Then, use a knife to cut the dough into bite-sized squares. Use a fork to poke the dough to make holes. This will help the cake to cook faster and more crispy.

3.Baking cake
Prepare to preheat the air fryer to 180 degrees Celsius for 5 minutes.

Next, spread the cut pieces of dough evenly on the baking tray.

Bake the cake for the first time at 160 degrees Celsius for 5 minutes.

Then, turn the cake over a second time at the same temperature until the cake is golden and crispy.

4.Finished product
Oatmeal Black Sesame Cookies with a crispy dough layer with a subtle, delicious smell of oats and the characteristic flavor of black sesame promises to be an "addictive" cake.

If you are in the diet phase, then this is a good candidate because you can consider this cake as a healthy, nutritious snack when you feel sad. Go to the kitchen and do it right away!

Tips for successful implementation:
Each type of oven has a different baking temperature difference. You can fix it to bake better by using an oven thermometer or by monitoring the cake regularly to adjust the temperature, baking time and baking groove accordingly.

How to preserve delicious and crispy cookies for a long time:
Cakes in a sealed bag or box, with an additional desiccant bag, can be used for 2-3 weeks. You should make the cake according to the instructions for the cake to be crispy and delicious.

Mint Butter Cookies

Ingredients for Mint Butter Cookies

- All-purpose flour 180 gr
- Mint leaves 30 gr
- Margarine 80 gr
- Vanilla powder 5 gr
- Baking powder 5 gr
- 1 chicken egg
- Powdered sugar 80 gr

Distinguish mint leaves and basil leaves

Although both are herbaceous plants, mint leaves are more pointed, larger in size, and have hairy surfaces. In contrast, basil leaves have a gourd shape and a hairless surface.

The veins and leaf flesh of mint leaves are equally prominent, while in basil leaves, the veins are more sunken than the flesh of the leaves.

Mint leaves have a cool, spicy aroma, similar to the taste of chewing gum. As for basil leaves, it has a light aroma, a faint spicy taste, not as strong as mint.

Implementation tools
Oven, whisk, hand blender, bowl, spoon,...

How to make Mint Butter Cookies

1.Grind the mint mixture
Mint picks carefully, remove dead leaves, worms, remove branches, take leaves and wash them.

Outward remittance:
If you don't have powdered sugar, you can replace it with pureed white granulated sugar.
You can replace the hand blender by putting the ingredients in a regular blender and puree.

2.Sieve and mix flour
Next, you sifted 90g of flour and then put it in a bowl of mint mixture, using a whisk to beat the mixture until it becomes smooth, smooth and wet.

At this time, continue to sift the remaining 90g of flour through a sieve and then put it in a bowl, add 5g of vanilla powder, 5g of baking powder and then continue to use a whisk to beat the mixture until it becomes a paste. special is okay.

3.Shaping and baking
Preheat the oven at 2 fire mode, 180 degrees Celsius for 10 minutes.

You prepare a baking tray, lined with a piece of parchment paper. Use a spoon to scoop a little dough into your hand, roll it into a ball, put it on a tray, then gently press the dough ball down with your hand, do the same until all the dough is gone.

To make the slices look better, put a fork in the water and press it back and forth across the surface of the dough, doing the same for the rest of the slices.

Finally, you put the cake tray in the middle of the oven, bake at 180 degrees Celsius, 2 fire mode for 15 minutes.

4.Finished product
That's it, the delicious mint butter cookies are done! Let the cake cool for 10 minutes and then transfer to a plate to enjoy.

Crispy, delicious cookie slices. The slightly fatty taste of the cake adds a bit of mint, combined with a cup of herbal tea, it's really "suitable for your age"!

Salted Egg Cookies

Ingredients for Salted Egg Cookies

- Salted Eggs 5
- All-purpose flour 190 grams
- Milk powder 30 grams

- Baking powder 1/4 teaspoon
- (baking powder)
- Unsalted butter 120 grams
- (let soften at room temperature)
- Powdered sugar 60 grams
- 1 chicken egg

How to choose to buy ingredients
The better the margarine, the better the cake will be, don't use margarine, the cake will not be as delicious.
The butter needs to be softened at room temperature but not to the point of mushy or watery.
Powdered milk is an optional ingredient, but it is highly recommended because milk will make the cake more fragrant and soft.
Ingredients for salted egg biscuits and salted egg biscuits with egg cream

Implementation tools
Oven, egg beater

How to make Salted Egg Biscuit

1. Preparing salted egg yolks
Separate the salted eggs, separate the yolks and discard the whites (the whites are very salty, but not as nutritious as the yolks). Rinse each yolk under running water gently to remove the viscous outside of the yolk.

Prepare a pot of boiling water, add salted egg yolks and cook for about 20 minutes over high heat. After steaming is complete, mash the salted egg yolks and let cool completely.

2.Make salted egg cookie dough
Sift 190 grams of flour, 30 grams of milk powder and baking powder into a large bowl.

Mix together flour, milk powder, and baking powder (mixture A).

In another large bowl, put the butter in the bowl.

Then, sift 60 grams of powdered sugar until smooth into the bowl of butter.

Use an electric mixer to beat the mixture on low speed, then gradually increase to medium speed, beat until the butter and sugar are combined, and the sugar has completely melted into the butter.

You beat until the butter is smooth, then stop.

Put the whole salted egg yolk puree into the bowl of butter. Continue using the mixer on low speed until the mixture is combined.

Divide the flour mixture (mixture A) into 2-3 equal parts, sift each part into the butter bowl. Use an electric mixer on the lowest speed until the flour is just combined, then add the next part of the flour mixture and continue beating in the same way until all the flour is combined.

Small tips:

If you don't have powdered sugar (icing sugar), you can use white granulated sugar and grind it fine. Regular granulated sugar can also be used, however, it will take a long time to mix the butter and sugar.

You only beat until the flour is just enough to blend with the butter, then stop, do not beat too long will make the butter melt, the cake will not be delicious.

3. Shape the cake

Use your hands to shape the dough into a smooth, elastic mass, out with parchment paper.

Put the dough on stencils and shape it by rolling it out and then using a cutter to shape the cake or you can also shape the dough into evenly round balls (20 grams/piece) as shown.

Separate 1 chicken egg, take the egg yolk.

Beat 1 egg yolk and add 1 teaspoon (5ml) of fresh milk, then use a brush to brush a very thin layer of that egg mixture on top of the cake and sprinkle with white or black sesame seeds as you like. delicious and beautifully colored.

Place the dough on a tray lined with parchment paper.

4.Baking cake
Preheat oven to 165 degrees C, two heat.

You put the cake tray in the oven at 160 degrees Celsius for about 18 - 20 minutes.

The finished cake will be very fluffy and soft, you leave the cake tray to cool and harden, then move the cake onto the rack and let it cool completely. So salted egg biscuits succeeded.

5.Finished product
Salted egg biscuits are both beautiful and strange to the mouth. Delicious biscuits with the salty taste of salted eggs, the rich aroma of black sesame, just hearing it is really attractive, right?

Salted Egg Cookies Egg Cream

Ingredients for making Salted Egg Cookies with Egg Cream

- Butter 100 gr
- Powdered sugar 60 gr
- Salted egg yolks 4 pieces
- Cake flour number 8 155 gr
- Milk powder 20 gr
- Baking powder 1/4 teaspoon
- Egg yolk 2 g
- Black sesame 10 gr

How to make Salted Egg Cookies with Egg Cream

1. Preparing salted eggs
Separate the salted egg yolks from the whites and rinse them under running water gently to remove the slime.

Next, put the salted egg yolks in the steamer for about 20 minutes, then take out the salted eggs and mash them finely.

2. Beat butter and sugar
Unsalted butter, cut into small pieces and leave at room temperature until the butter is soft, then put the butter in a bowl with 60g of powdered sugar, use a hand mixer to beat the butter and sugar together until the mixture turns pale yellow. turn white then stop.

3. Mix the dough
Put the salted egg yolks in a bowl of butter and sugar, beat them with an electric mixer until well combined.

Sift 155g of 8th cake flour, 20g of powdered milk and 1/4 teaspoon of baking powder into the bowl of salted egg mixture. Use a spatula to mix well and then beat with an electric mixer.

Next, use your hands to knead the mixture into a smooth dough, no longer sticking to your hands.

4. Shape the cake
Divide the dough into 24 parts, roll each part into a ball. In the middle of the ball, use your finger to press it down. Place the dough balls on a baking tray lined with non-stick baking paper.

Beat the egg yolks and then scoop a little into the indentation in the center of the cake. Next, sprinkle some black sesame seeds on top of the cake. You do this one at a time until you run out of ingredients.

5. Baking cake
Preheat the oven for 10 minutes at 170 degrees Celsius to stabilize the temperature.

Put the cake tray in the oven at 160 degrees Celsius for 15 minutes, the cake is cooked.

6.Finished product
Crispy biscuits with the aroma of roasted sesame, salty and fatty, the taste of salted egg yolk is extremely attractive. Enjoy the cake with some hot tea is the best!

Tips for successful baking

Each type of oven has a different baking temperature difference. You can fix it to bake better by using an oven thermometer or by monitoring the cake regularly to adjust the temperature, baking time and baking groove accordingly. Freshly baked cakes will be frizzy and fragmented, but after about 5-7 days of being stored in an airtight container, the cake will be more delicious.

Store the cake in a sealed bag or box, with an additional desiccant bag. If stored well, the cake can be used for 2-3 weeks.
You should make the cake according to the instructions for the delicious crispy cake.
How to choose to buy delicious salted eggs
Delicious salted eggs on the outside will have no stretch marks, no mold spots, gently shake the egg to feel that there is little water inside.

Looking at the eggs under the light, the egg whites are clear, pink, the egg yolks are miniature, and close to the shell is a delicious egg.

If you peel an egg and see that the egg white is thin, the yolk is pink, small and slightly sticky, you should buy it.

Do not buy if the egg white is opaque, the yolk is thin, has a bad smell.

Salted Egg Nougat Cookies

Ingredients for Salted Egg Nougat Cookies

- Cookies 24 pieces
- Unsalted butter 60 gr
- Cooked salted egg yolk 45 gr

- Sugar 5 gr
- Milk powder 9 gr
- Marshmallow 90 gr
- Green onions, chopped 2 plants

How to make Salted Egg Nougat Cookies

1.Mix the onion butter mixture
Put in a bowl 30g melted unsalted butter, 5g sugar, 2 chopped scallions and stir until the sugar dissolves.

2.Sweet cookie butter
Using a brush, spread a thin layer of the onion butter mixture over each cookie.

Next, you sprinkle some more onions on top of the cake, then pan-fry the cake on low heat until the surface is dry and slightly golden.

Pro tip: You can bake the cake in the oven at 150 degrees Celsius for 10 minutes. If using an air fryer, you should lower the temperature a little bit about 130 - 140 degrees Celsius.

3.Make salted egg nougat filling
Finely mash 45g of cooked salted egg yolks through a sieve.

Finally, add 9g of powdered milk, continue to mix until the candy mixture is blended, slightly thickened.

Outward remittance:

It is recommended to cook the butter and marshmallow mixture over the lowest heat.

It is recommended to use an electric stove or an infrared stove to cook, not a gas stove because it will cause the mixture to burn quickly and the finished product to harden.
It is recommended to use a non-stick pan to cook the candy so that the candy does not stick to the pan.

4.Cake tongs
Put the salted egg candy mixture into the whipped cream bag, then you pump the cream into the center of the inside of the cookie.

Next, place another cookie on this piece of candy, let the cake cool completely before enjoying.

Tip: Letting the candy cool a bit will make it easier to pump the filling, because the candy will be a bit thick at this point, so it won't melt.

5.Finished product

The biscuits have a crispy crust, fragrant with the smell of onion butter, fatty leopard flesh mixed with soft and sweet soft candy filling, with a characteristic salty taste from salted eggs, extremely delicious and not boring at all.

How to preserve cakes?
Put the cake in an airtight bag or an airtight container, store at room temperature, cool for 1-2 weeks.

Chocolate Chip Mochi Cookies

Ingredients for Chocolate Chip Mochi Cookies

- All-purpose flour 160 gr
- (wheat flour number 11)
- Glutinous rice flour 70 gr
- Cornstarch 20 gr
- Cocoa powder 15 gr
- Coconut oil 20 gr
- Unsalted Butter 113 gr
- Chocolate chips 40 gr
- Brown sugar 70 gr
- White sugar 30 gr
- Fresh milk without sugar 140 ml
- Baking salt 1/2 teaspoon
- (baking soda)
- 1 chicken egg
- Salt 1/4 teaspoon
- Vanilla essence 1/2 teaspoon

Implementation tools
Oven, microwave, mixer, bowl, stencils,...

How to make Chocolate Chip Mochi Cookies

1.Make chocolate chips
Melt the dark chocolate, then place in a piping bag.

Next, squeeze on the wax paper many small cones equivalent to the size of chocolate chips and then let the chocolate harden.

Pro tip: If you have chocolate chips on hand, you can skip this step.

2. Beat the butter

Puree 113g unsalted butter until soft, then add 70g brown sugar, 15g white sugar and stir until the butter is white.

Next, you add 1 egg, 1/2 teaspoon of vanilla essence and continue to stir until the mixture thickens.

Tips for combining brown sugar and white sugar to create a delicious cake texture:

Brown sugar will make the cake more sweet, soft and fragrant. The white sugar will help the cake achieve a firm crunch. Therefore, you should combine both types of sugar with the above quantity to give the cake a better texture.

In case you lack one of the two types of sugar, they can be used interchangeably with the same quantity. However, this will cause the texture of the cake to be different.

3. Mix the cookie dough

Put in a bowl 160g finely sifted flour, 1/4 teaspoon salt, 1/2 teaspoon baking soda and mix well.

Then, you add the dry flour mixture to the butter mixture and mix well to combine.

When the mixture is mixed, add 15g of finely sifted cocoa powder and continue to mix well.

Next, add 40g of chocolate chips, mix well one more time and you're done.

Finally, cover the dough with cling film, place it in the refrigerator for 30 minutes to 1 hour.

4.Make the mochi
Put in a bowl 70g glutinous rice flour, 20g cornstarch, 15g sugar, 140ml fresh milk without sugar and stir until the mixture is smooth.

Cover the bowl with cling film, then microwave at 800W for 1 minute 30 seconds.

After 1 minute 30 seconds, you mix the dough well and continue to spin for another 1 minute 30 seconds to cook.

When the dough is cooked, add 20g of coconut oil and then knead the dough with your hands until the coconut oil is mixed.

Pro tip: If you don't have a microwave, you can steam the dough for 30 minutes over medium heat!

5. Shape the cake

Divide the cookie dough into parts, 20g each, and then roll them into balls.

For the mochi cake, you also divide it into several pieces with a weight of 10g and then roll them up.

Use your hands to flatten the cookie dough, then put the mochi filling in the middle, pinch the edges of the dough and round it, slightly flatten it.

Next, use some chocolate chips to stick on top of the cake.

6. Baking cake

Preheat a 2-fire oven to 180 degrees Celsius.

Put the cake in the oven, bake at 180 degrees C, center groove for the first 9 - 10 minutes.

Then, lower the oven temperature to 160 degrees Celsius and bake for another 3-4 minutes.

7. Finished product

The finished cake has a soft, spongy crust, sweet and bitter with cocoa flavor and greasy with butter flavor, the inside is chewy and chewy, both strange and extremely delicious.

How to preserve cakes?

Let the cake cool completely, put in an airtight container or bag and store in the refrigerator for 3-5 days. When eating, just reheat in the microwave for about 5 seconds.

Button Cookies

Ingredients for the Button Cookies

- All-purpose flour 200 gr
- (wheat flour number 11)
- Unsalted Butter 125 gr
- Powdered sugar 80 gr
- 1 chicken egg
- Vanilla essence 1 little
- Salt 2 gr

Implementation tools
Egg beater, oven, bowl, mixer, small round mold

How to make Button Cookies

1. Beat butter with sugar
Put in a bowl 125g unsalted butter, 80g sugar and then use a butter beater.

Then, you add 1 egg and continue to use the mixer to blend.

Outward remittance:

Butter needs to be softened at room temperature, pressed with your hands to be soft enough but not to the point of mushy or watery.

2.Mix cake dough
Put in a bowl of butter 120g flour, 2g salt, 1 little vanilla essence and mix well until the flour is combined, forming a mass.

Spread the dough evenly in cling film and place in the fridge for 2 hours.

3.Shaping buttons
Divide the dough into several pieces, then roll them into balls and roll them out.

Use a bottle cap to cut the dough, then use a smaller round mold to press the inside contour.

Next, use a small straw to make 2 small holes to resemble buttons.

Repeat until the remaining dough is used up.

4.Baking cake
Preheat oven to 180 degrees C for 10 minutes.

Prepare a baking tray lined with parchment paper, then place the cake and bake at 180 degrees C for 15 minutes until golden brown.

5.Finished product
Biscuits have lovely buttons, try a crispy piece that melts in your mouth, sweet, fatty, extremely delicious.

How to preserve cakes?
Let the cake cool completely, put in a sealed bag or sealed jar and store for 1 month.

Cinnamon Bean Cookies

Ingredients for making Cinnamon Bean Cookies

- Chickpeas 200 gr
- All-purpose flour 100 gr
- (wheat flour number 11)
- White sugar 67 gr
- Vanilla essence 2 teaspoons
- Unsalted butter 1 tbsp
- Condensed milk 76 gr
- 1 chicken egg
- Egg yolk 1 pc
- 1 little baking soda
- (baking salt)
- Cinnamon powder 1 tbsp
- Sesame seeds 1 little
- 1 pinch salt
- Water 473 ml

Implementation tools
Oven, pot, mixer

How to make Waffles with Beans

1. Cook beans
Softly soak 200g of mung beans for 12-24 hours, then remove the seed coat and wash the beans.

When the water in the pot foams, stir continuously until the foam dissolves, then lower the heat to medium and cook until the beans are tender.

2. Puree the beans

Puree the beans, stir until the water in the pot is dry and the beans are thickened.

Then, add 67g of white sugar, 1 pinch of salt, 1 teaspoon of vanilla essence. Mix well over low heat until completely blended.

Let the beans cool, cover and place in the fridge for 1 hour.

3. Mix cake dough

Melt 1 tablespoon unsalted butter, then add 76g condensed milk, 1 little baking soda, 1 pinch of salt, 1 egg, 1 teaspoon vanilla essence. Stir to combine the mixture.

Add 100g of flour and continue to stir until the mixture is thick and smooth.

Cover the dough and let rest for 1 hour.

Note: If the mixture is still liquid, you can add a little more flour.

4. Shape the cake
Coat the dry dough evenly on the cake dough, then divide it into 2 equal parts. Similarly, you also divide the bean paste into 2 parts and then round.

Roll the dough, spread it evenly into a circle, put the bean paste in the middle and then pinch the edge of the dough.

Roll each piece of cake, coat evenly through cinnamon powder and then cut into bite-sized pieces.

5. Baking cake
Preheat oven to 175 degrees Celsius for 15 minutes.

Stir in 1 egg yolk, then spread it on the white part of the cake, sprinkle with a little sesame to finish.

Bake for 20 minutes at 175 degrees Celsius.

Note: Remember to place the cake at a distance from each other, because the cake will expand even larger than the original size.

6. Finished product
The finished biscuits have a strong aroma of cinnamon, have a crispy crust, are extremely thin, and the bean paste is sweet and soft, blended with the crispiness and characteristic taste of toasted sesame. The cake will be more delicious when you serve it with tea.

3 Flavor Cookies Whole Wheat Flour

Ingredients for 3 Flavor Cookies with Whole Wheat Flour

- Whole wheat flour 400 gr
- Honey 195 ml
- Coconut oil 180 ml
- (or butter)
- Dark Chocolate 70 gr
- Cocoa powder 35 gr
- Almond flour 50 gr
- Chia seeds 20 gr
- Strawberry 150 gr
- Chicken eggs 3
- Almond milk 30 ml
- Fresh milk 40 ml
- Baking powder 1/2 teaspoon
- (Leavening)
- Salt 1/2 teaspoon
- Vanilla essence 1 teaspoon
- 1 handful of almonds

How to make 3 Flavor Cookies with whole wheat flour

1.Mix the butter cookie dough
Put in a bowl 400g whole wheat flour, 1/2 teaspoon salt, 1/2 teaspoon baking powder and mix well.

In a new bowl: 150g honey, 180ml coconut oil, 1 teaspoon vanilla essence, 2 eggs. Stir to combine the mixture.

Add the honey mixture to the bowl of dry flour and mix well until the dough is sticky and incorporated. Divide the dough into 3 parts: 1 part 200g and 2 parts 300g.

2.Mix the macaroons
In a new bowl: 200g flour mixture, 50g almond flour, 1 beaten egg and mix well. Then put this powder into the whipped cream bag.

3.Mix chocolate cake powder
Mix well the mixture of 30g cocoa powder, 30ml almond milk, 15ml honey.

Put in a new bowl: 300g of flour mixture, cocoa mixture and mix well.

Pro tip: If the mixture is too wet, you can add a little more dry powder.
4.Make strawberry jam
Put the pot on the stove, add 150g of strawberries, 30ml of honey. Cook over low heat until strawberries are soft.

Then, add 20g of chia seeds, mix well, then use a spoon to puree the strawberry jam, turn off the heat and let it cool.

5.Make chocolate filling
Heat a mixture of 70g dark chocolate, 40ml fresh milk, 5g cocoa powder and mix well in a water bath.

Pro tip: If the mixture is still liquid, you can add a little cocoa powder.

6. Shape the cake

For the almond dough: Scoop the dough onto parchment paper, then place 1 almond nut on top of the cake.

For chocolate dough: Put the dough in between 2 sheets of parchment paper and roll it out until the dough has a thickness of 2-3mm.

For the remaining 300gr of dough mixture: Roll out similarly to a thickness of 2 - 3mm.

Put the remaining chocolate powder and flour mixture in the refrigerator for 1-2 hours.

Pro tip: At this point, you can bake the almond flour first. After cooling the dough, you begin to shape the remaining 2 parts of the dough.

Use a round mold to cut the dough, then use a smaller round mold to drill a hole inside.

Note: Only make a small hole in half of the cake.

7. Baking cake

Preheat oven to 170 degrees Celsius for 15 minutes.

Bake each cake at 160 - 170 degrees C for 15 - 20 minutes.

After baking, place the cake on a high rack to cool.

8.Decorate the cake
Spread the chocolate filling on the chocolate cake shell, then use a puff pastry bag to draw more lines on the cake.

Spread the strawberry jam on the butter cookie crust.

9.Finished product
3 eye-catching, fragrant and irresistible biscuits, delicious, crunchy almond cookies, bittersweet chocolate chip cookies and sweet and sour strawberry biscuits. Each type has its own unique attractive flavor, you will definitely like it!

Cinnamon Sugar Roll Cookies

Ingredients for Cinnamon Sugar Roll Cookies

- All-purpose flour 200 gr
- (wheat flour number 11)
- Cream cheese 50 gr
- (cream cheese)
- Unsalted Butter 80 gr
- Brown sugar 15 gr
- Cinnamon powder 1/2 teaspoon
- Powdered sugar 90 gr
- Chicken eggs 2
- Vanilla essence 1/2 teaspoon
- Milk powder 20 gr
- (optional)

Implementation tools
Oven, whisk, mixer

How to make Cinnamon Sugar Roll Cookies

1. Beat the butter
Using a mixer, beat 50g cream cheese and 80g unsalted butter on medium speed.

Next, add 90g of powdered sugar and beat at medium speed until the butter is soft and turns light yellow.

Stir in 1 egg, slowly add to the bowl of butter with 1/2 teaspoon vanilla and beat until combined.

2.Mix cake dough
Mix 200g all-purpose flour, 20g milk powder. Divide this mixture into 2-3 parts and then sift into the bowl of butter, using a mixer to mix well.

Cover the bowl of dough and place in the fridge for 30 minutes.

3. Shape the cake
Put the cake dough on a piece of parchment paper, fold this wax paper into a rectangle and make sure to cover the dough inside. Use the spreader to thin the dough inside so that it matches the size of the created rectangle.

Unfold the parchment paper, then sprinkle on top of the cake batter 15g brown sugar and 1/2 teaspoon cinnamon powder. Gently roll the 2 edges of the cake in the middle and then put it in the refrigerator for 30 minutes to harden the dough.

After 30 minutes, take the cake out and cut it into slices about 1/2 inch thick.

Finally, gently squeeze the bottom of the cake with your hands to create a heart shape.

4. Baking cake

Preheat oven to 180 degrees Celsius for 15 minutes.

Place the cake on a baking tray lined with parchment paper, stir in 1 egg yolk and spread it gently on top of the cake.

Put the cake in the oven and bake at 180 degrees C for 13 - 15 minutes until golden crispy.

5. Finished product

Cookies have a very cute shape, crispy, soft, melt in the mouth, sweet, fatty with a little warmth from delicious cinnamon powder.

How to preserve cakes?
Let the cake cool completely, place in an airtight container or sealed bag and store at room temperature for 1 month.

Cat Tongue Cookies

Ingredients for Cat Tongue Cookies

- Flour No. 8 25 g
- Egg whites 25 gr
- Unsalted Butter 25 gr
- (let soften at room temperature)
- Powdered sugar 20 gr
- Vanilla essence 1 little

How to make Cat Tongue Cookies

1.Piece the butter mixture
Mash 25g unsalted butter, then add 20g powdered sugar, 1 little vanilla and mix well to blend.

2.Mix cake dough
Divide 25g egg whites and 25g flour into 3 parts.

First, you put 1 part egg white in a bowl of butter and mix well. Then, you add 1 part of the flour and continue to mix well.

Mix the ingredients like this until the rest is over, this will help the mixture blend more evenly.

3. Shape the cake
Line a baking sheet with parchment paper and then begin to shape the cake.

Put the flour mixture into the ice cream bag, squeeze the cream into pieces about 4 fingers long. Remember to leave a little distance, because the cake will expand when it's cooked.

4.Baking cake
Put a thick layer of salt in a pan, cover and heat.

When the salt in the pan is hot, put the cake tray in, close the lid and bake on medium heat for 7 minutes.

After 7 minutes, turn the cake over and bake for another 4 minutes and it's done.

5.Finished product
Cat tongue cake is cooked to a golden brown color, fragrant with butter, when eaten, the cake has a crispy texture with a sweet and fatty taste, extremely delicious.

Contents

- Peanut Butter Cookies — 5
- Brownie Cookies Cream — 8
- Brownie Cookie Matcha — 12
- Ginger Cinnamon Cookies — 16
- Cheese Seaweed Cookies — 20
- Almond Cookies Cereal — 24
- Cereal Cookies — 27
- Banana Peanut Butter Cookies — 30
- Raspberry Jam Cookies — 33
- Apple Cookies — 36
- Almond Green Tea Cookies — 39
- Eggless Soybean Cookies — 42
- Peach Cookies — 45
- Cherry Blossom Cookies — 49
- Cashew Cookies — 53
- Orange Cookies — 56
- Keto Lemon Cookies — 60
- Sweet Potato Cookies — 64
- Corn Cookies — 67
- Cheese Cookies — 72
- Almond Chocolate Keto Cookies — 75
- Chocolate Cookies — 79

- Coffee Bean Cookies — 83
- Chocolate Candy Cane Cookies — 88
- Banana Oatmeal Cookie Cookies — 93
- Oatmeal Black Sesame Cookies — 99
- Mint Butter Cookies — 104
- Salted Egg Cookies — 108
- Salted Egg Cookies Egg Cream — 113
- Salted Egg Nougat Cookies — 118
- Chocolate Chip Mochi Cookies — 122
- Button Cookies — 128
- Cinnamon Bean Cookies — 132
- 3 Flavor Cookies Whole Wheat Flour — 136
- Cinnamon Sugar Roll Cookies — 141
- Cat Tongue Cookies — 145

Printed in Great Britain
by Amazon